Dtp
and
graphic design

Iacob Adrian

Da Vinci

Plants

visual study

ISBN-13 : 978-1477643181

ISBN-10 : 1477643184

Iacob Adrian

2012

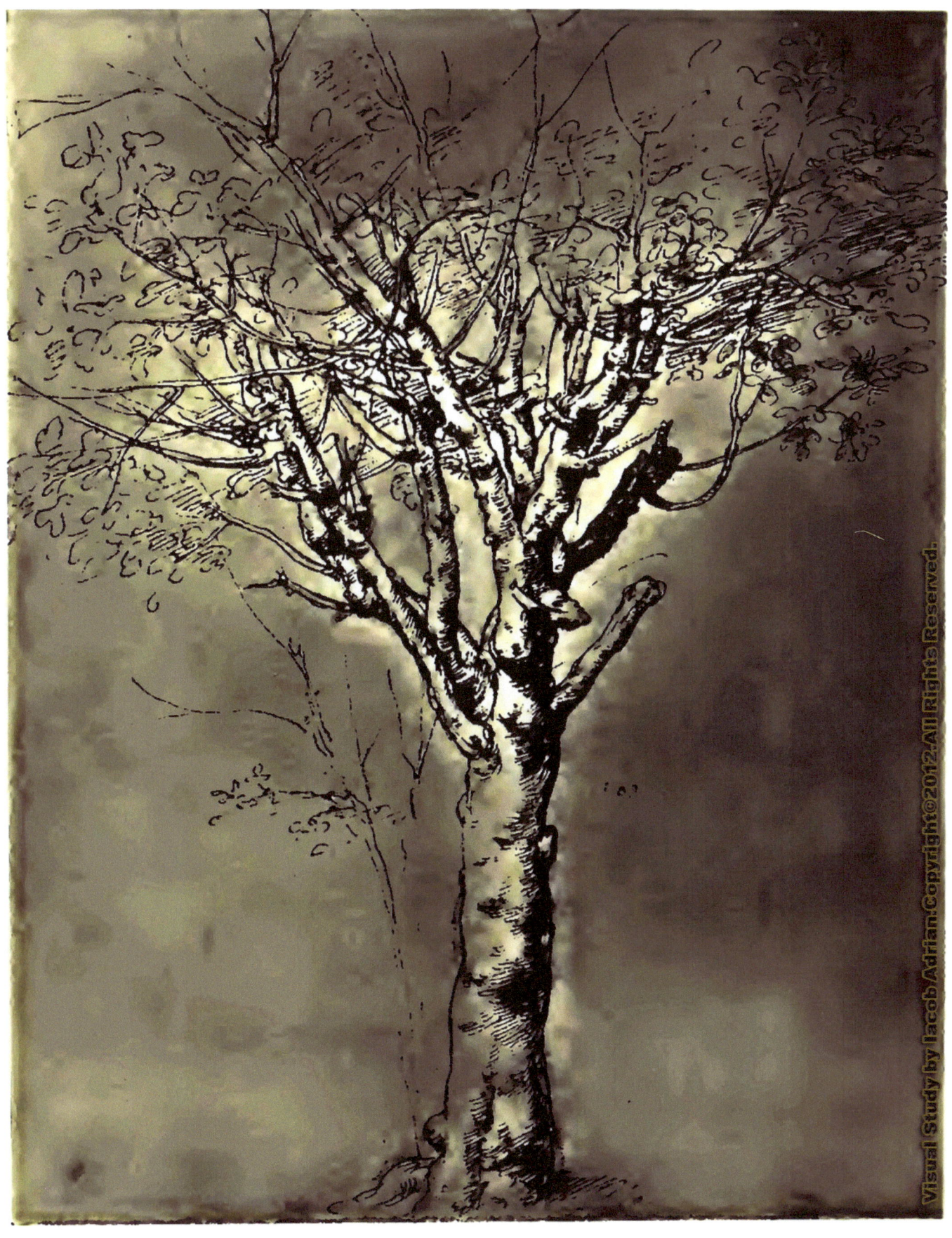

STUDY OF A TREE

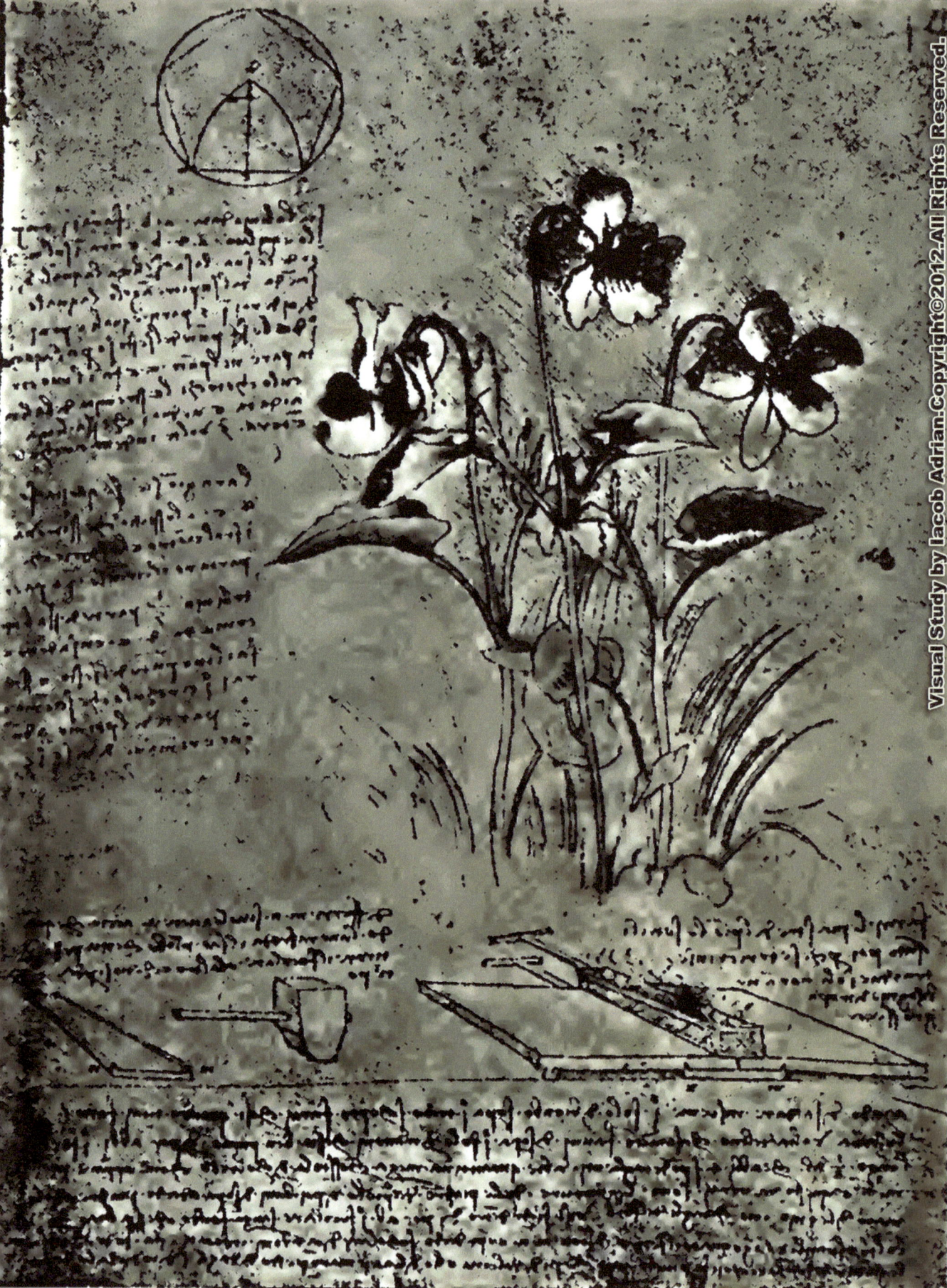

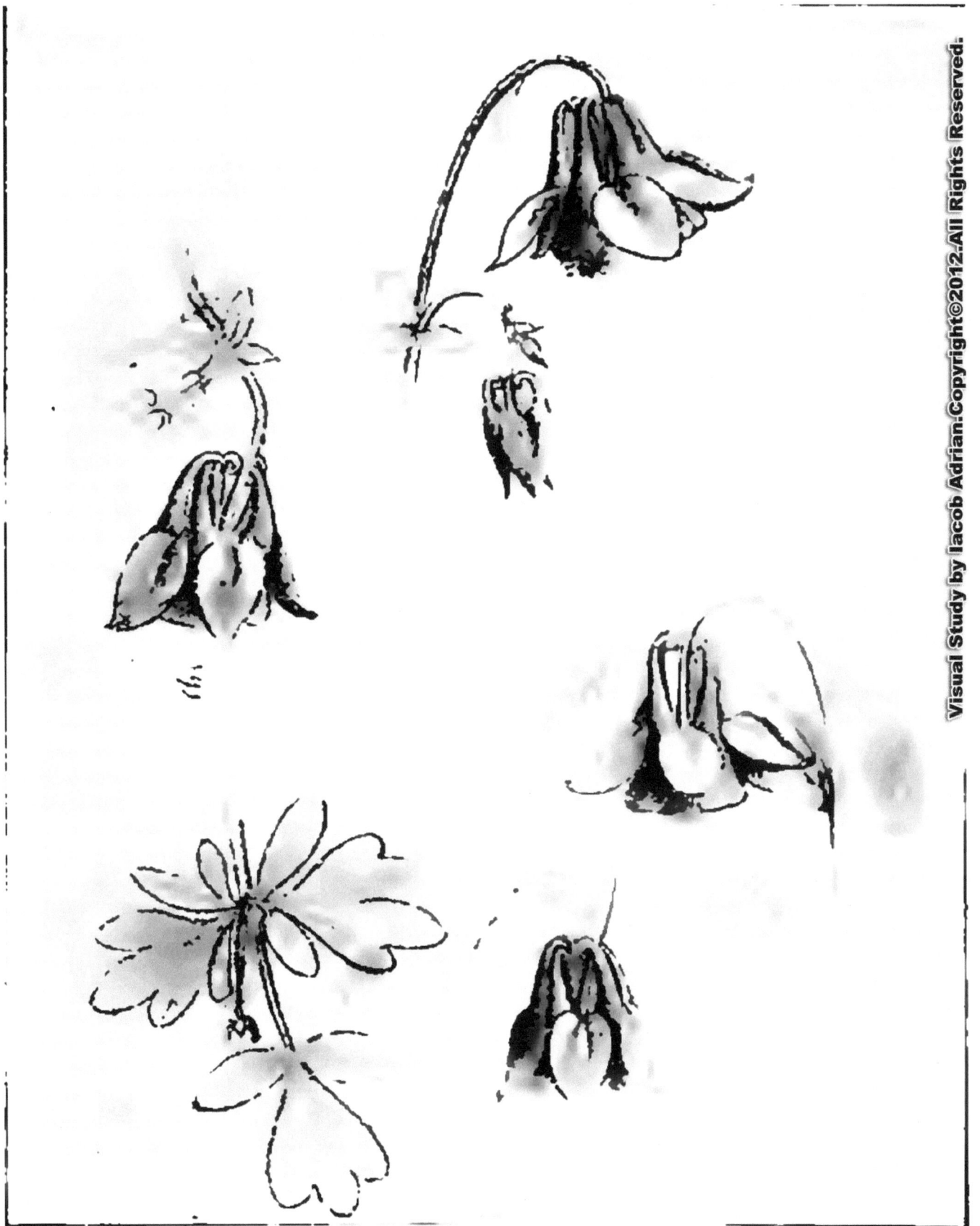

STUDIES OF FLOWERS AND LEAVES

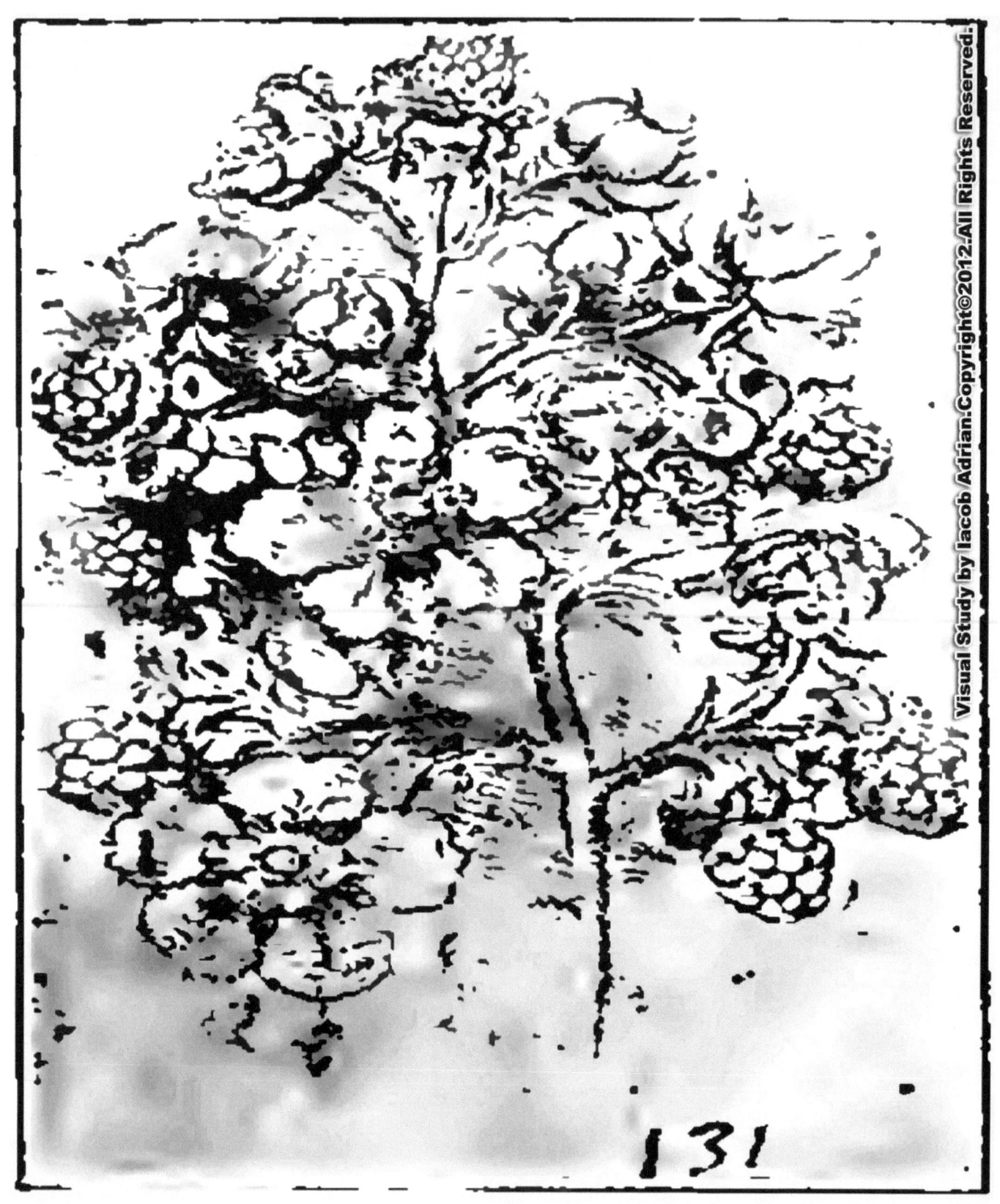

131

STUDY OF FLOWERS.

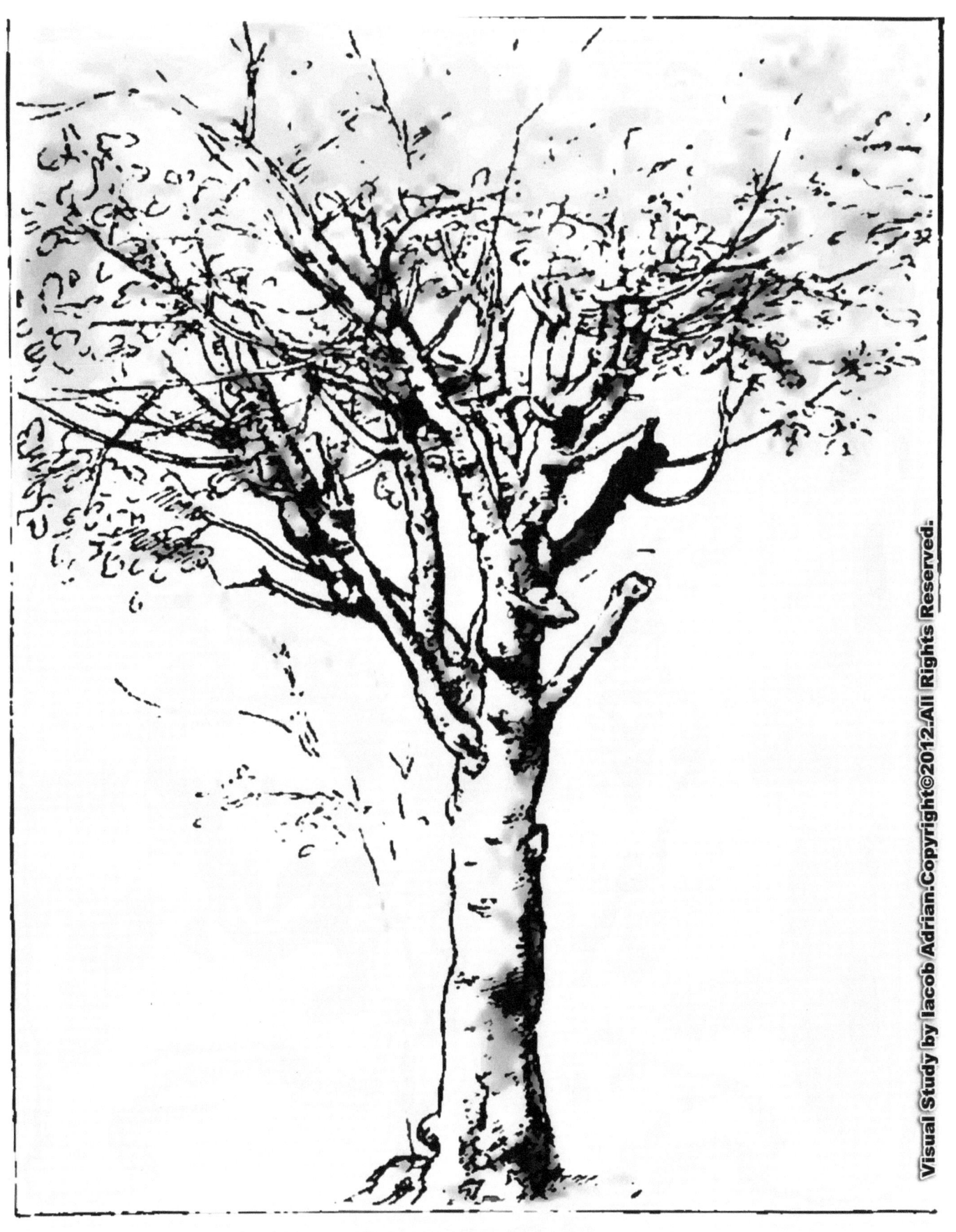

STUDY OF A TREE.

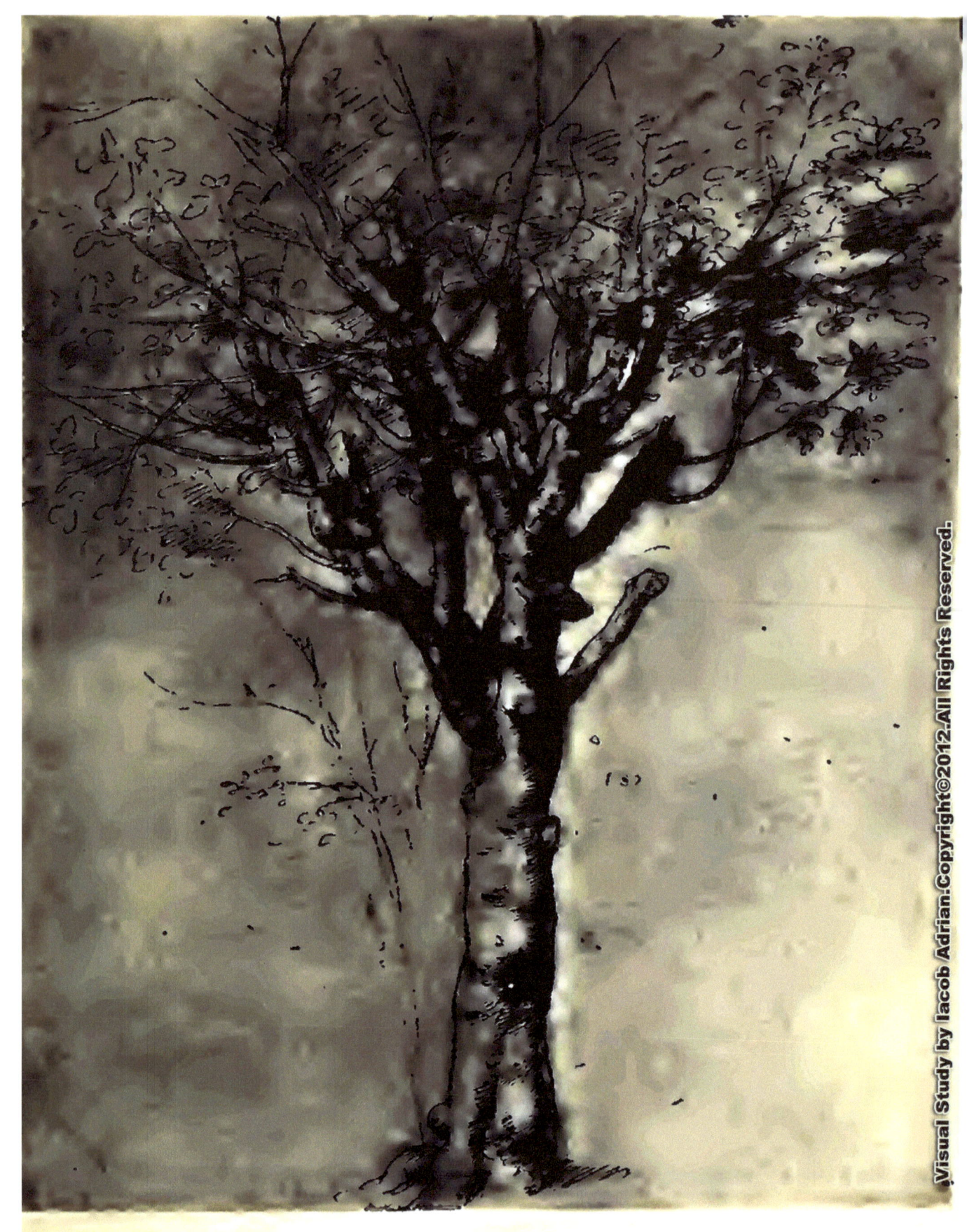

STUDIO DI ALBERO

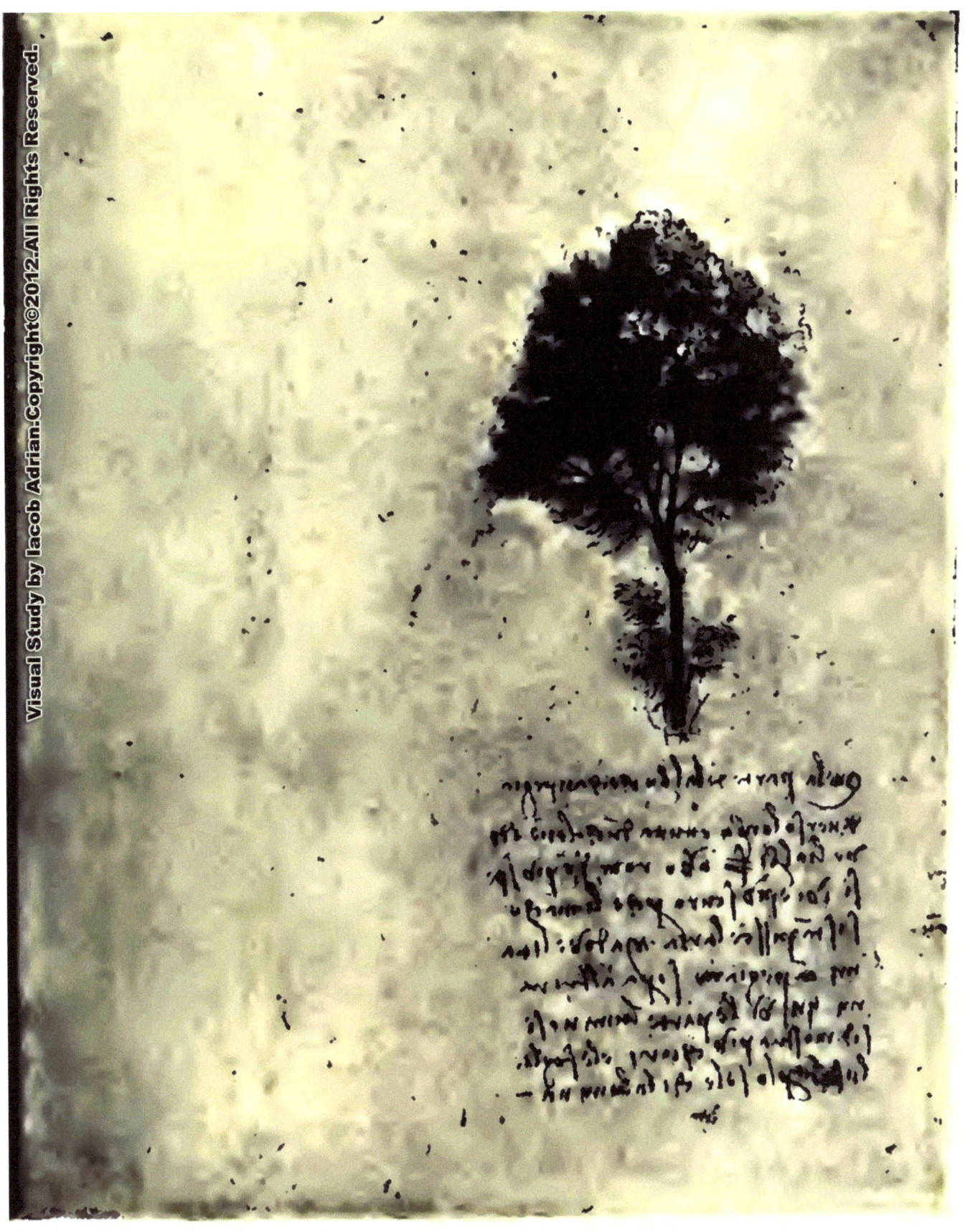

STUDIO DI ALBERO

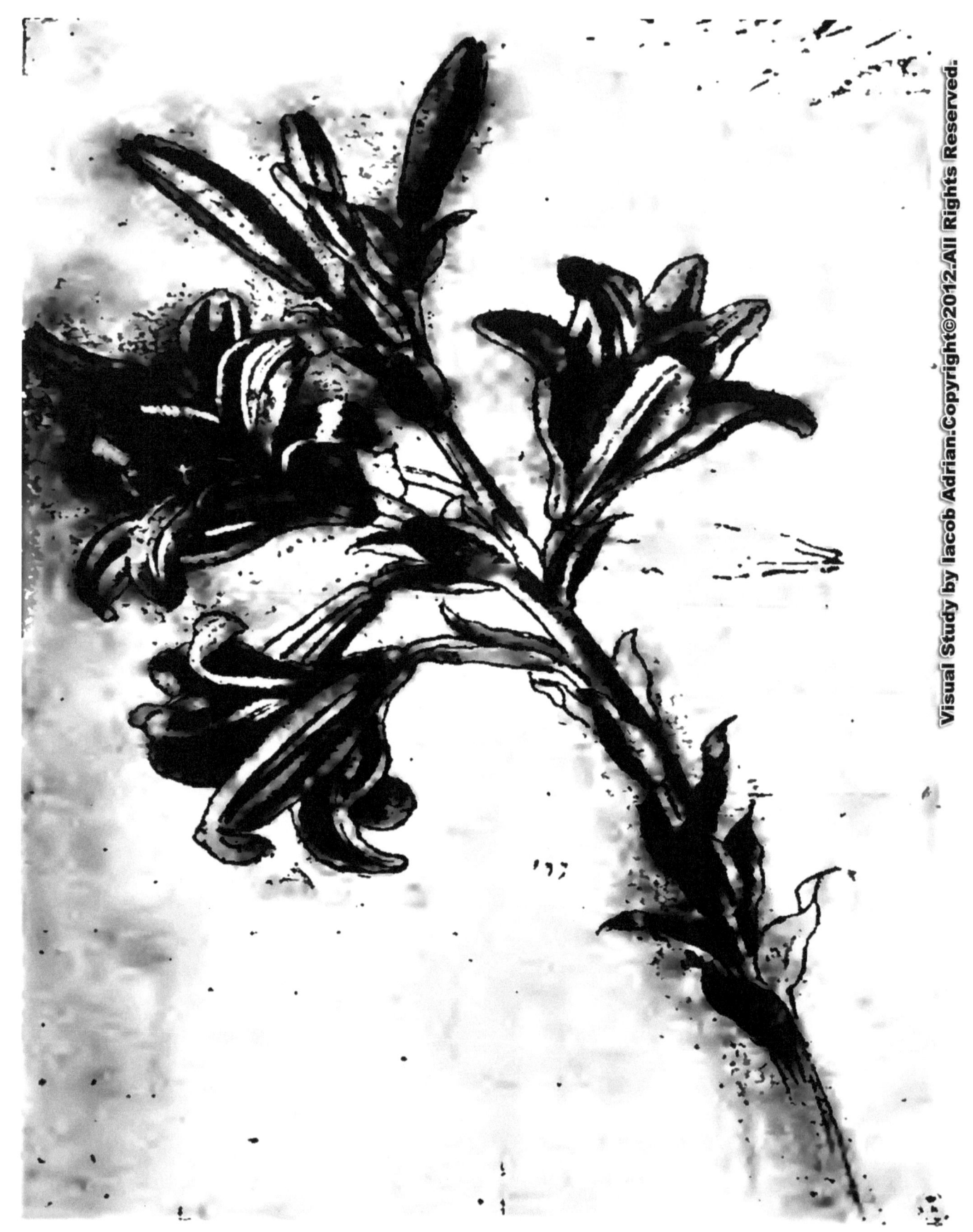

LILIUM CANDIDUM L.

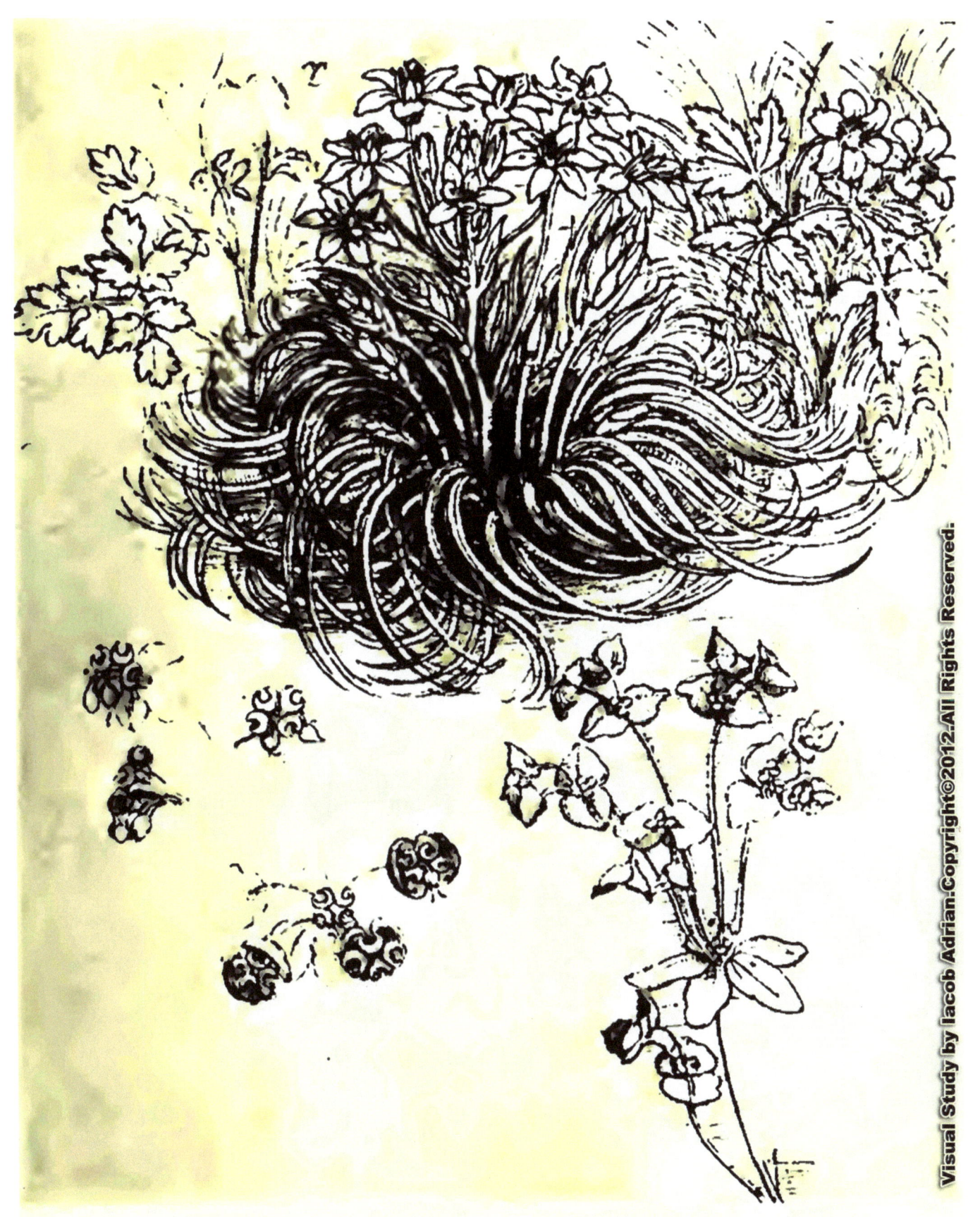

STUDI DI PIANTE ERBACEE

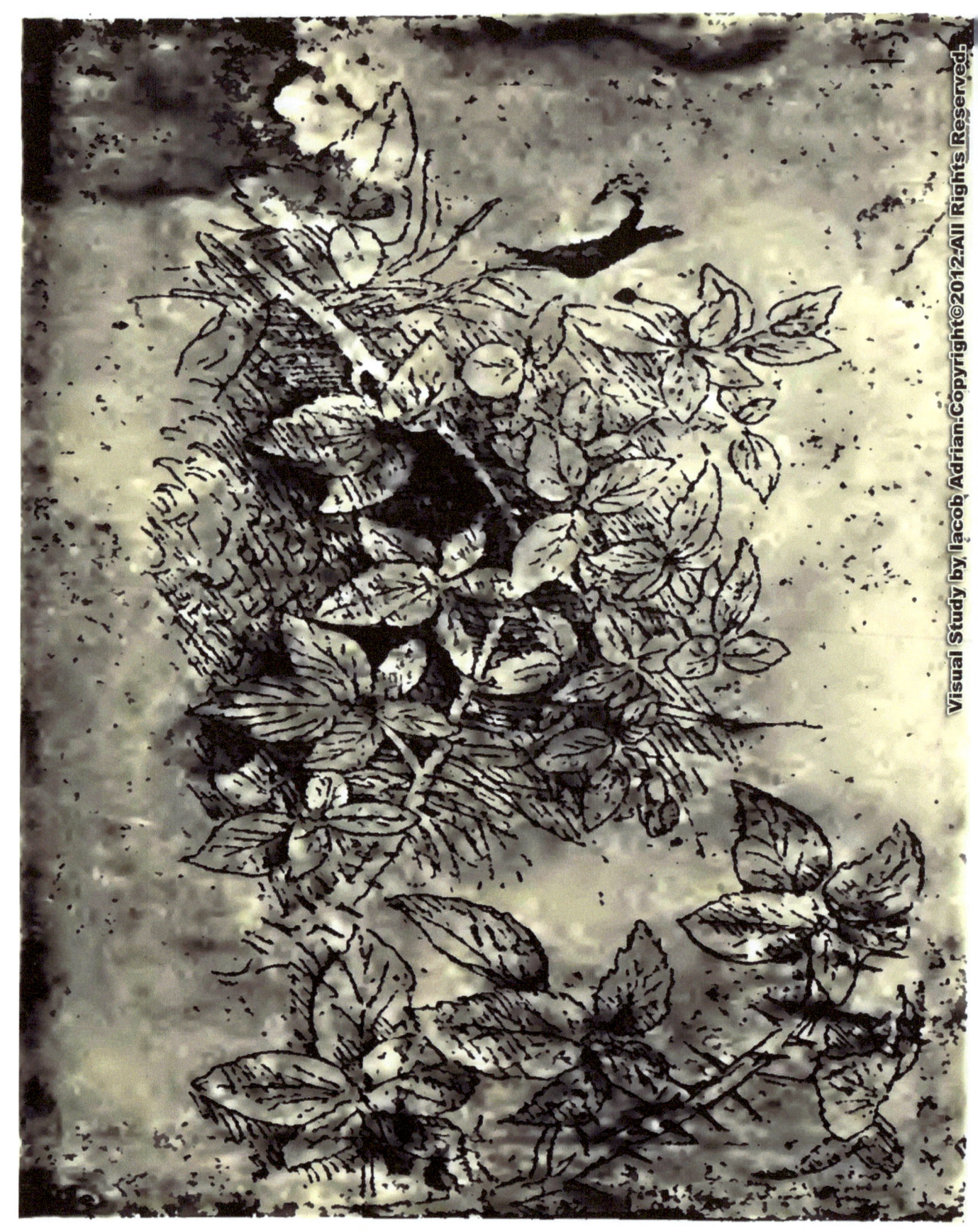

RUBUS FRUTICOSUS L.

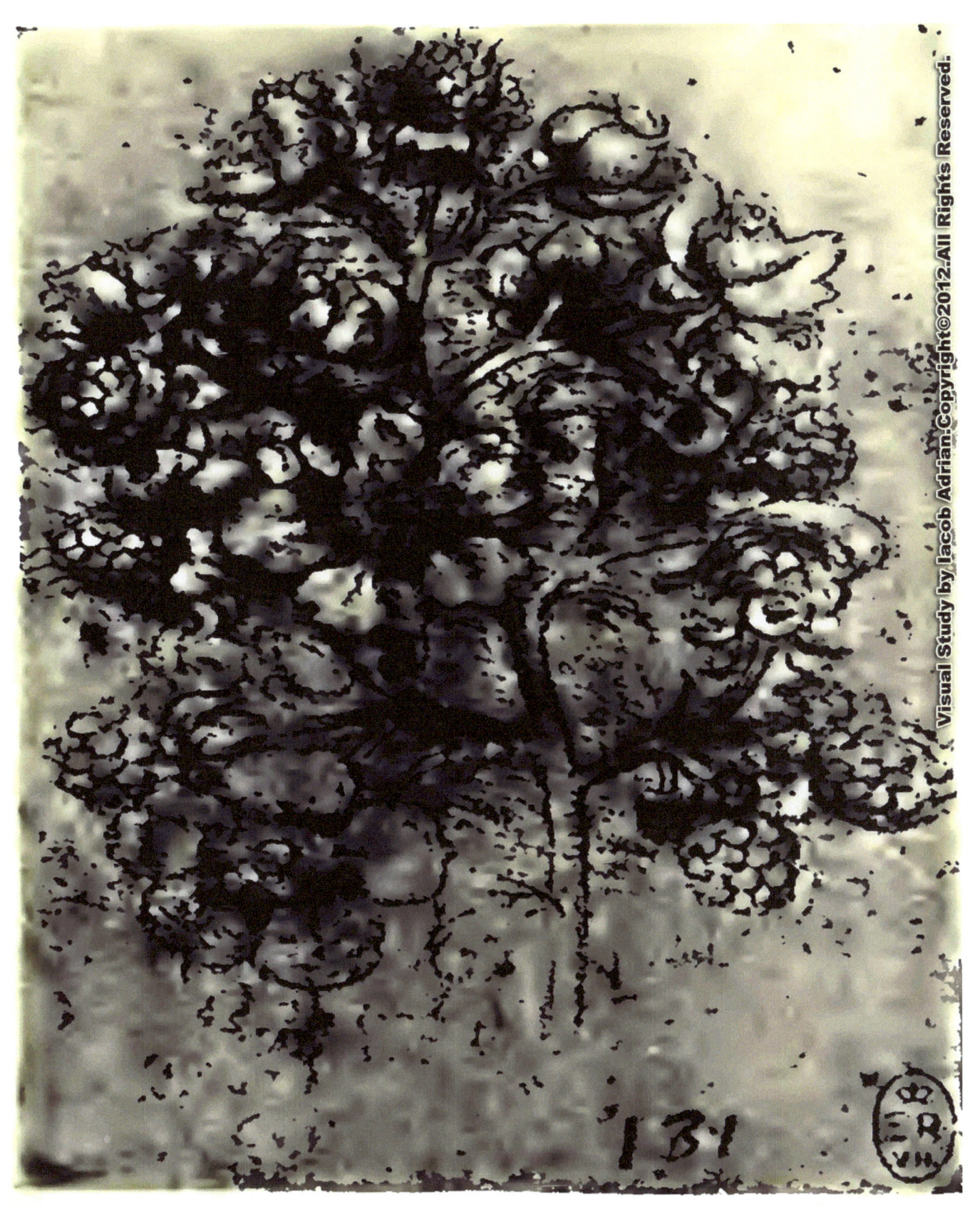

RUBUS FRUTICOSUS L.

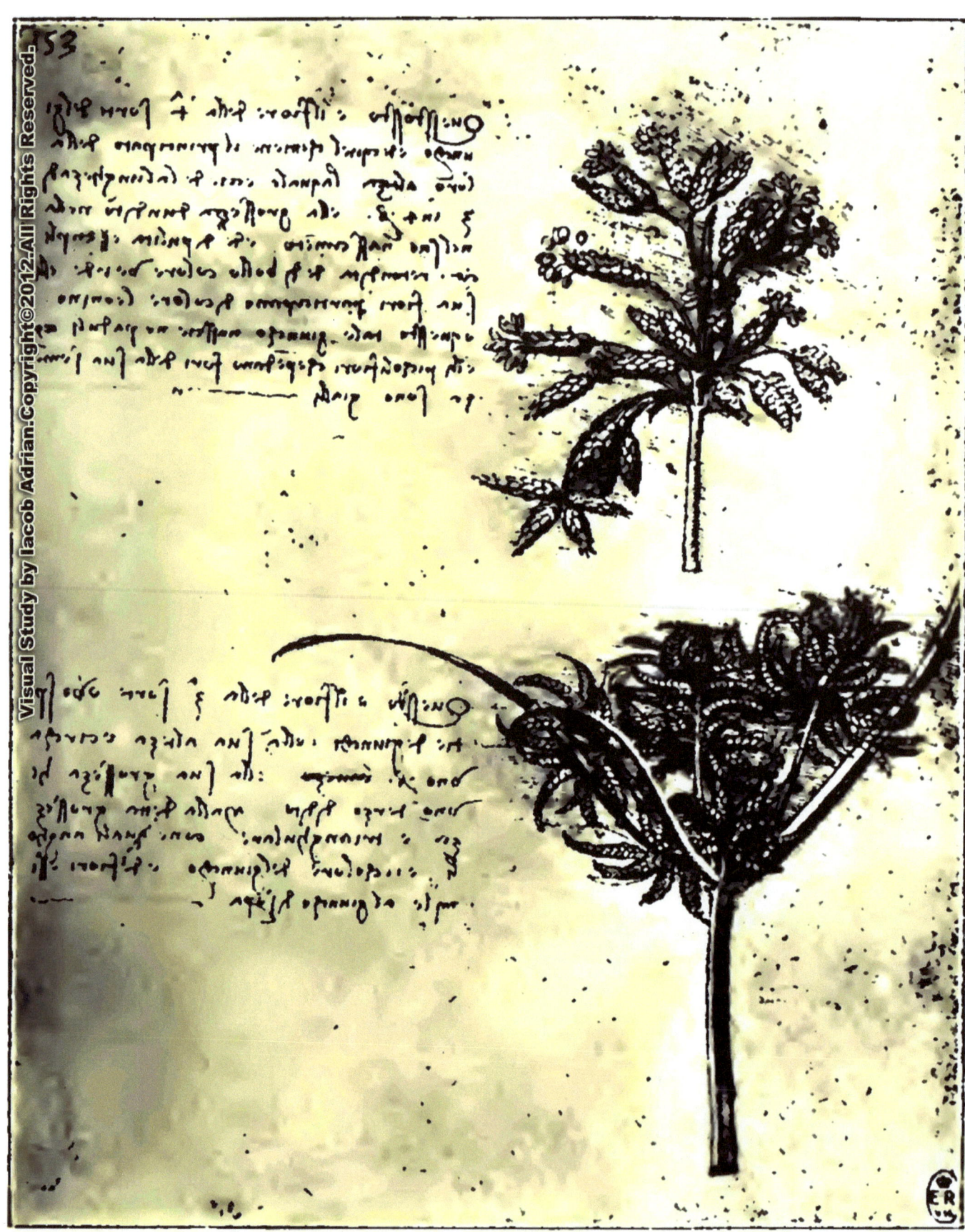

STUDI DI CIPERACEE

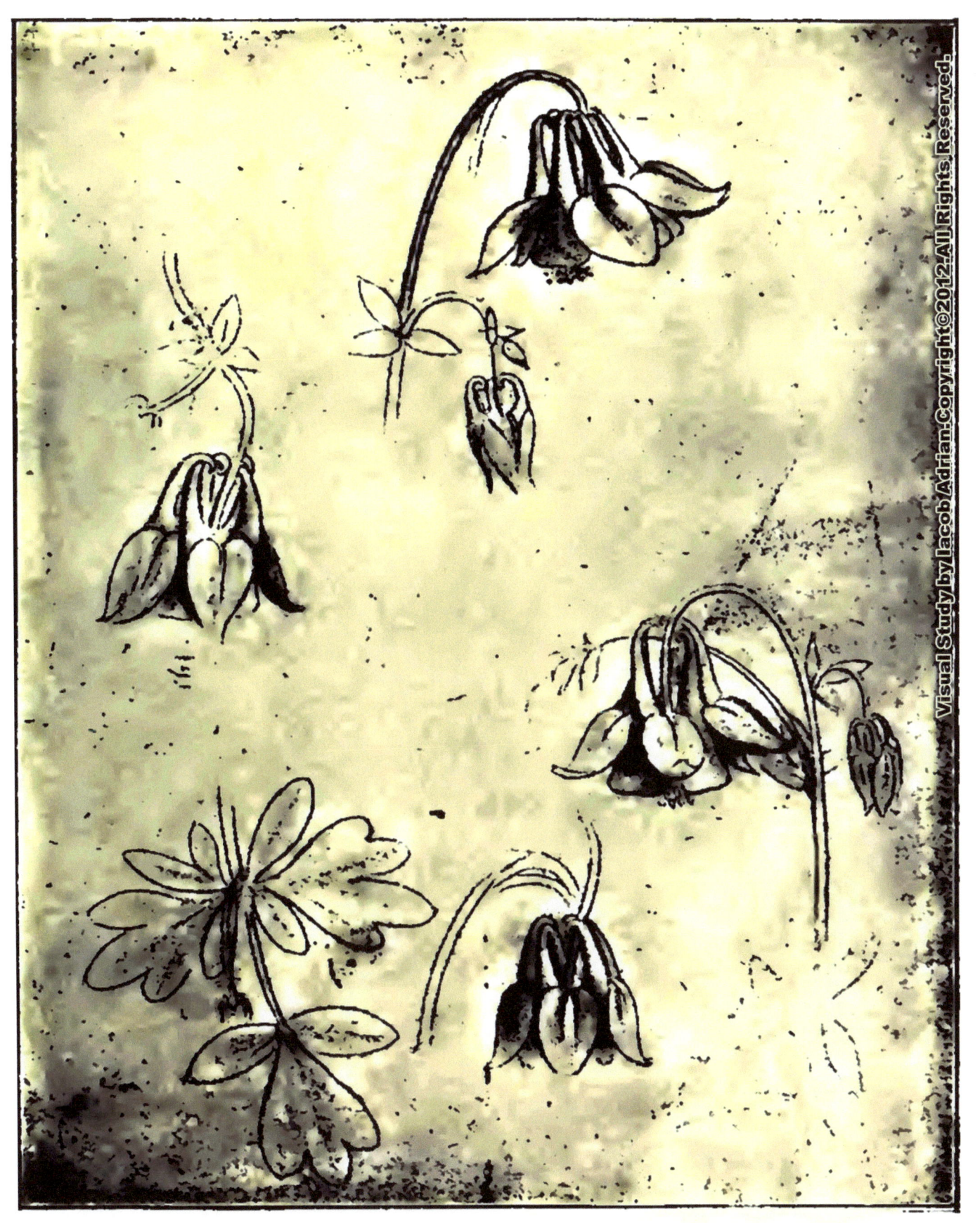

AQUILEGIA VULGARIS L.

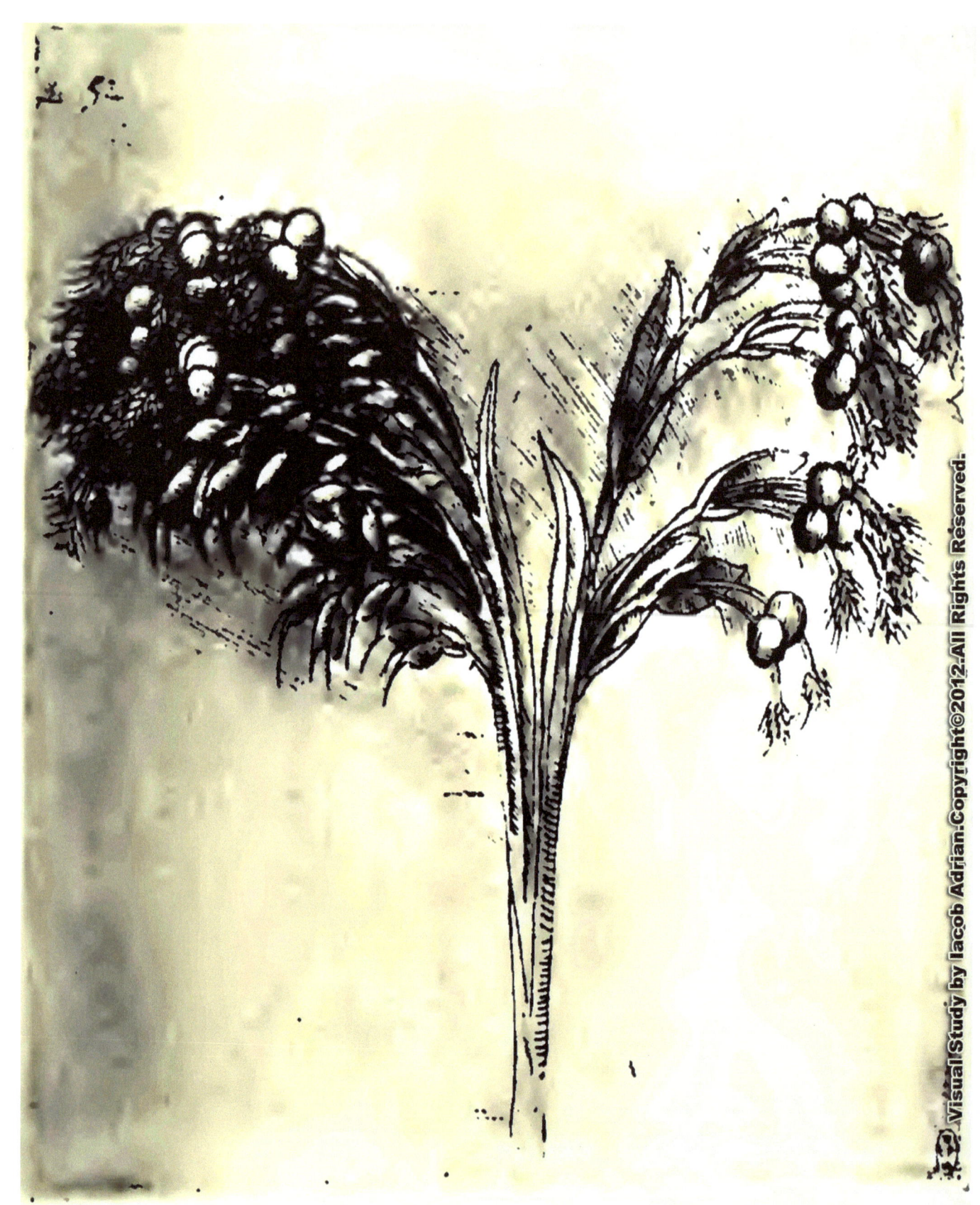

COIX LACHRYMA L.

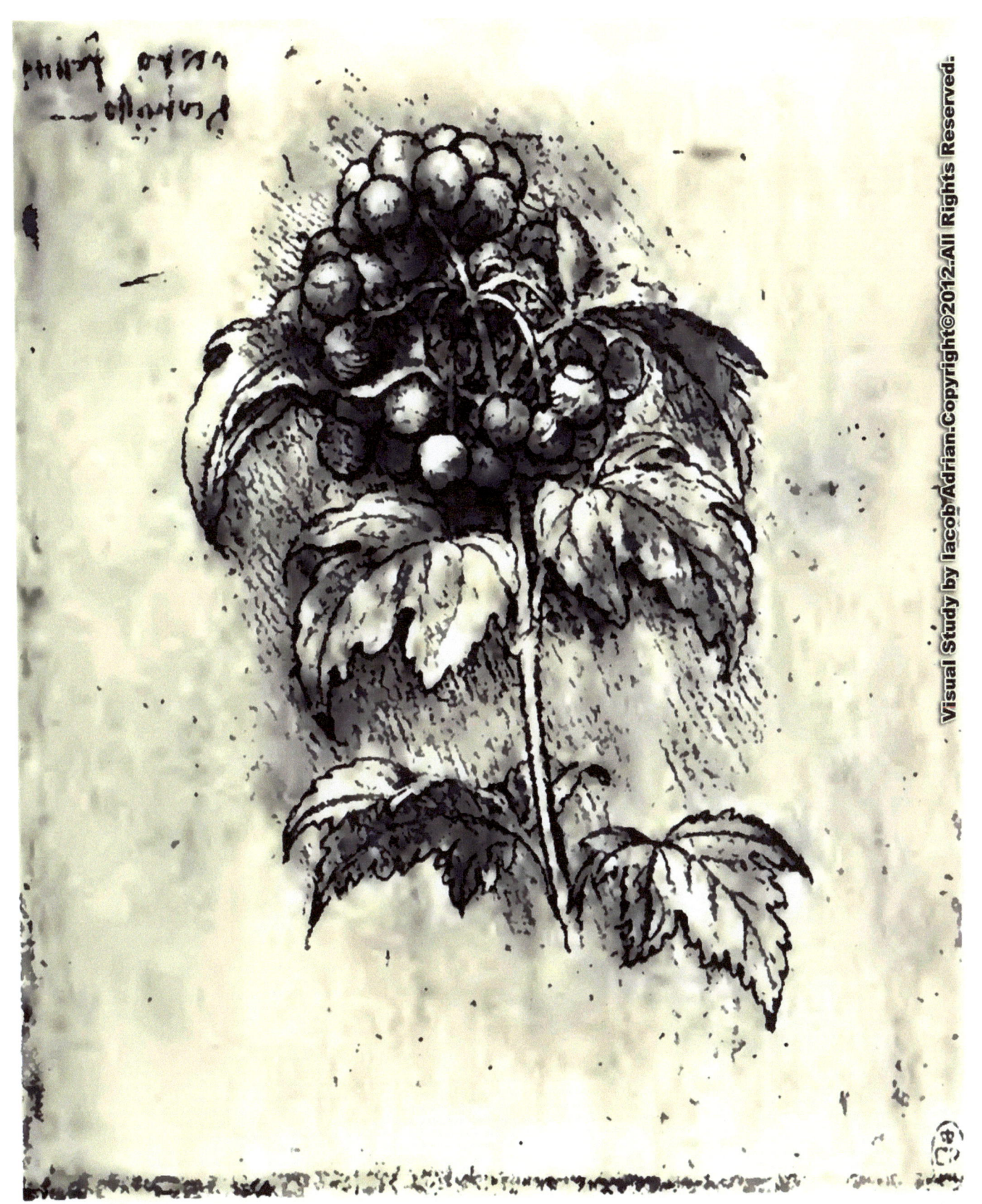

PYRUS TORMINALIS (L.) Ehr.

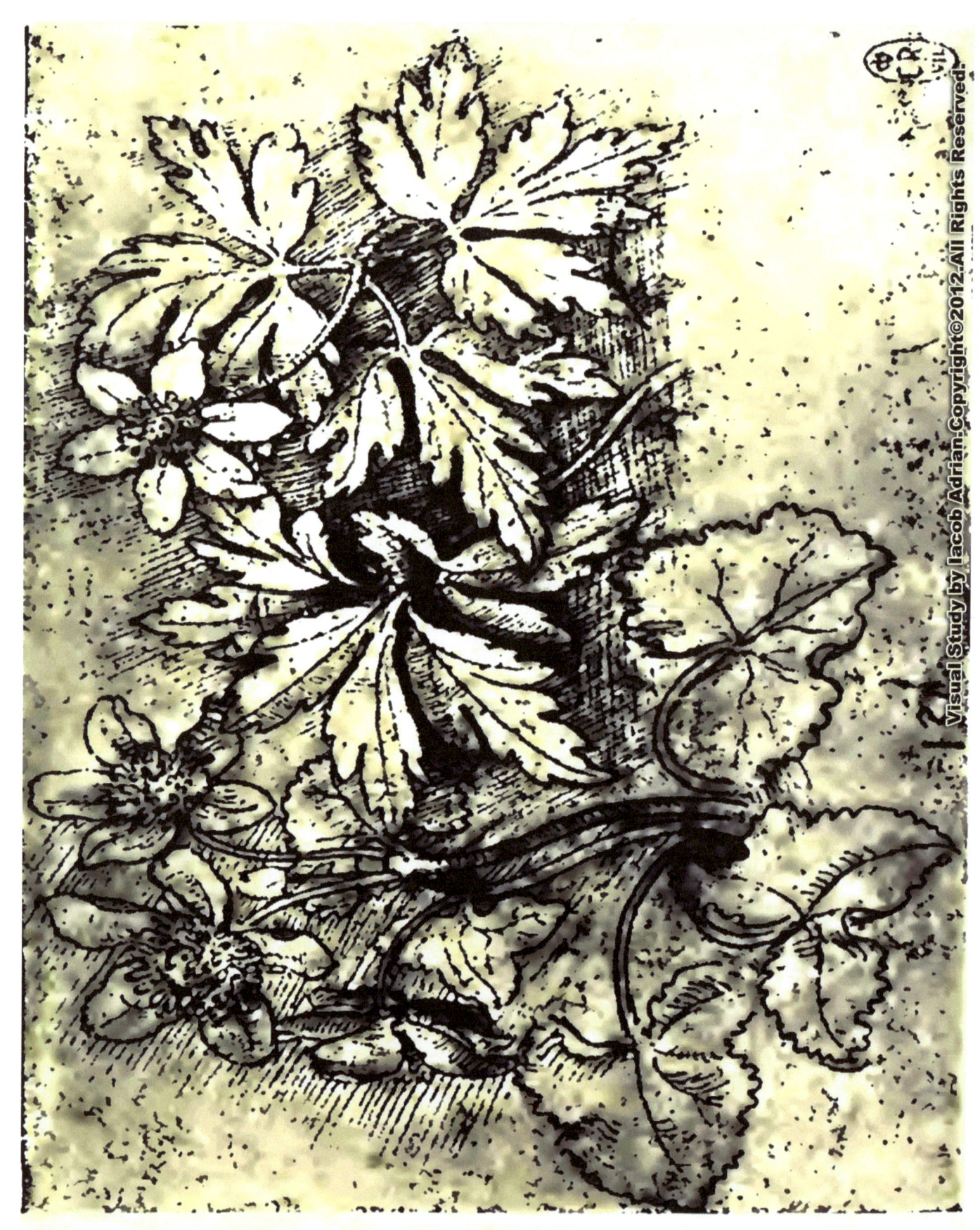

STUDI DI PIANTE ERBACEE

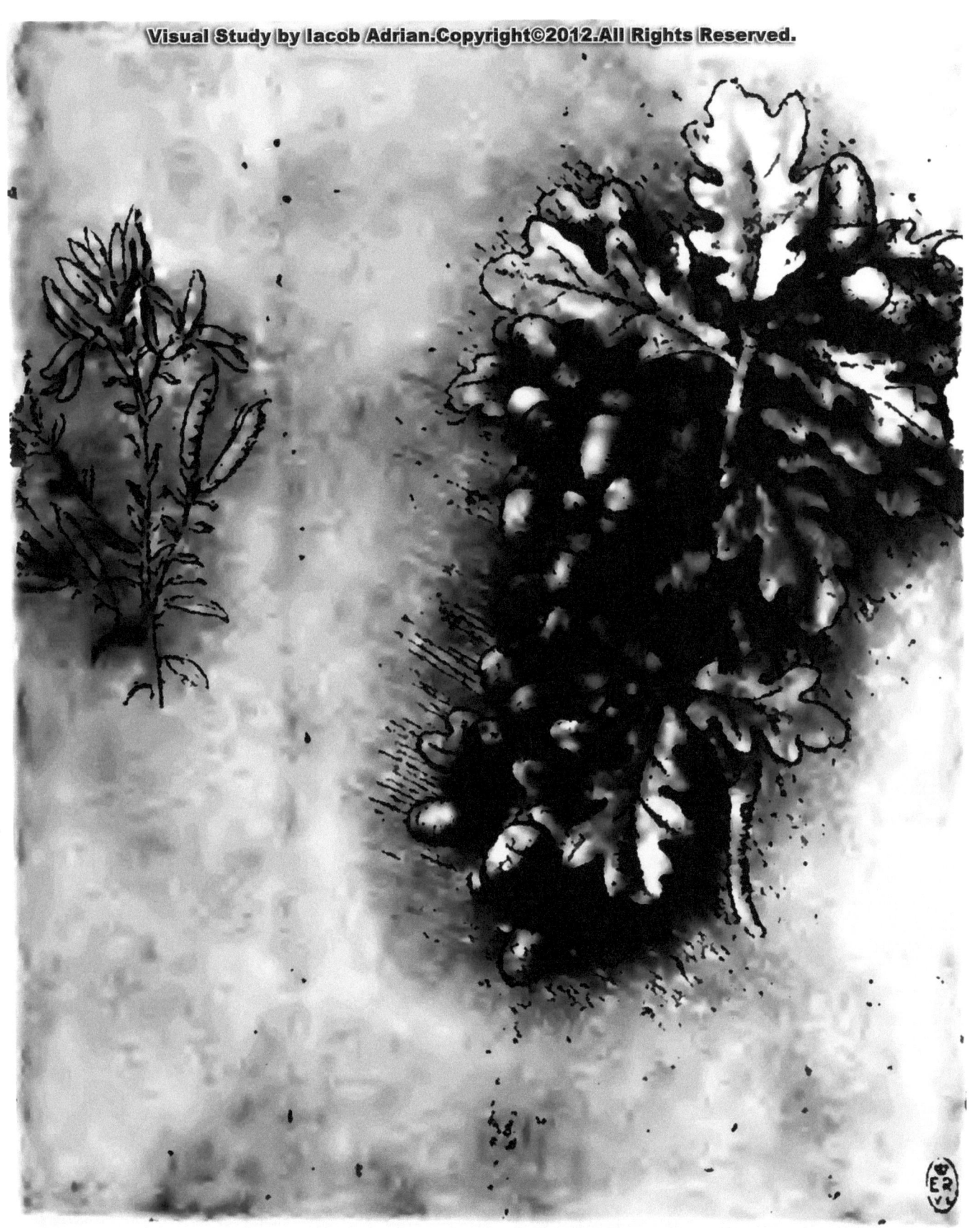

STUDI DI PIANTE

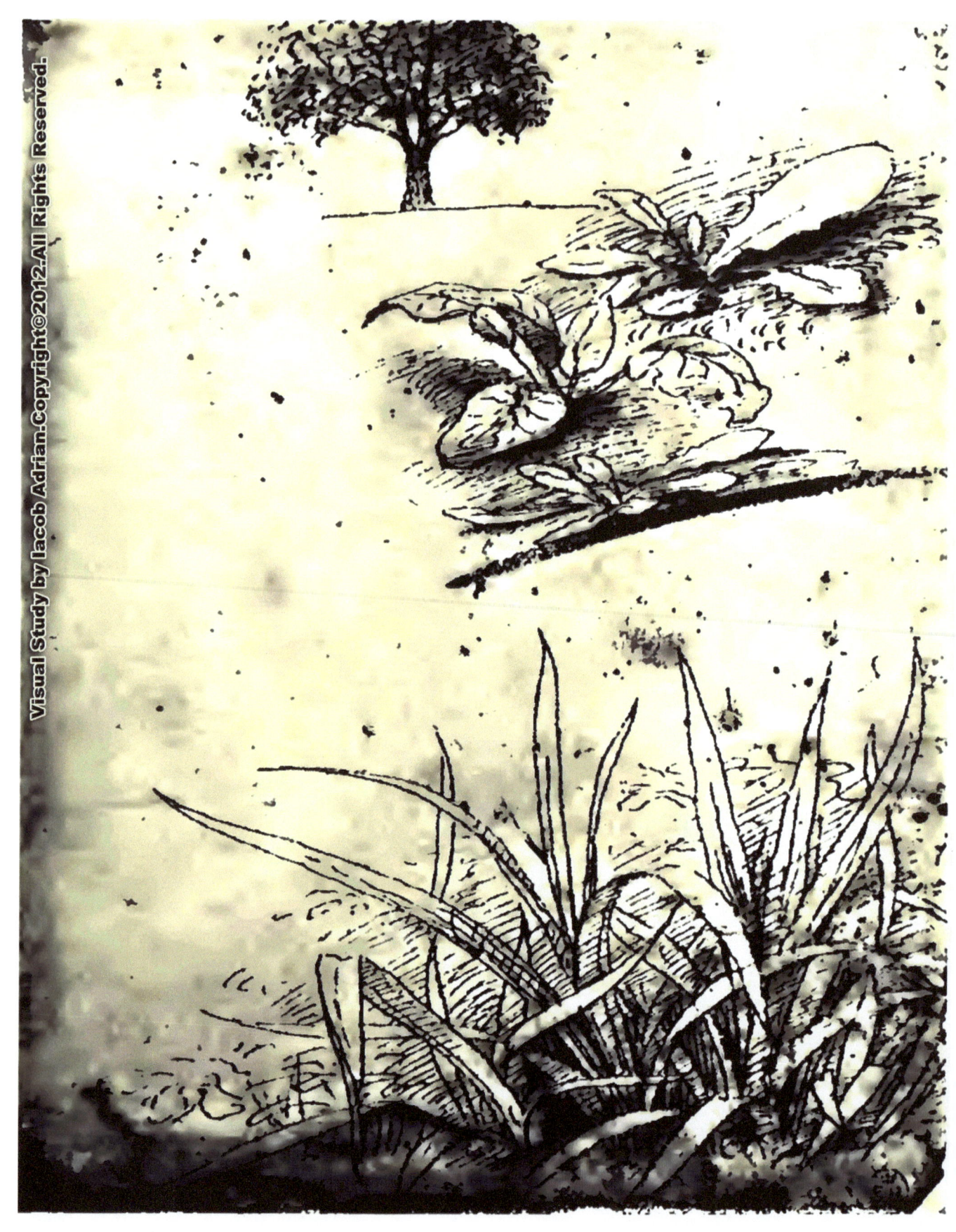

STUDI DI PIANTE LEGNOSE ED ERBACEE

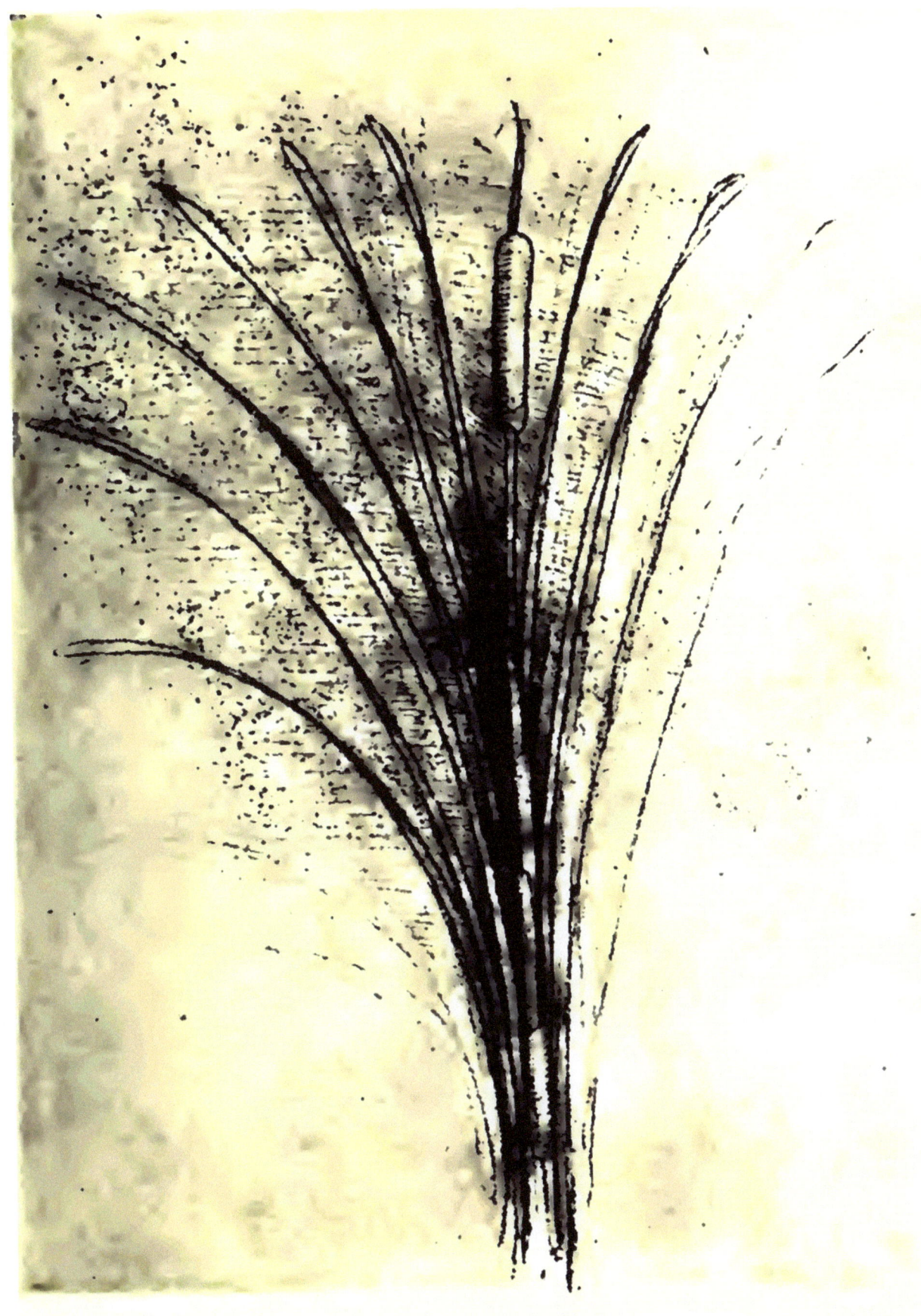

TYPHA LATIFOLIA L.

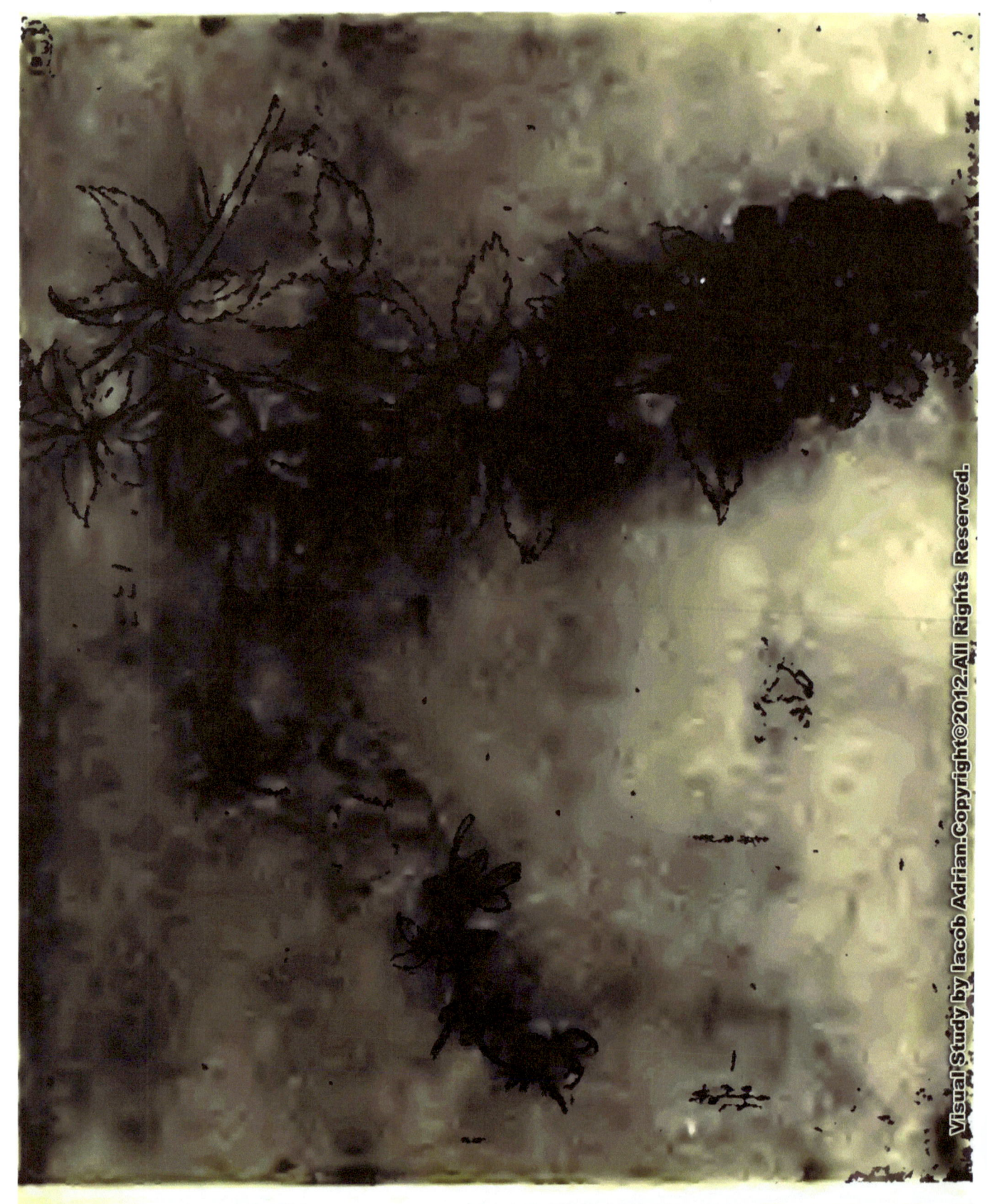

STUDI DI PIANTE

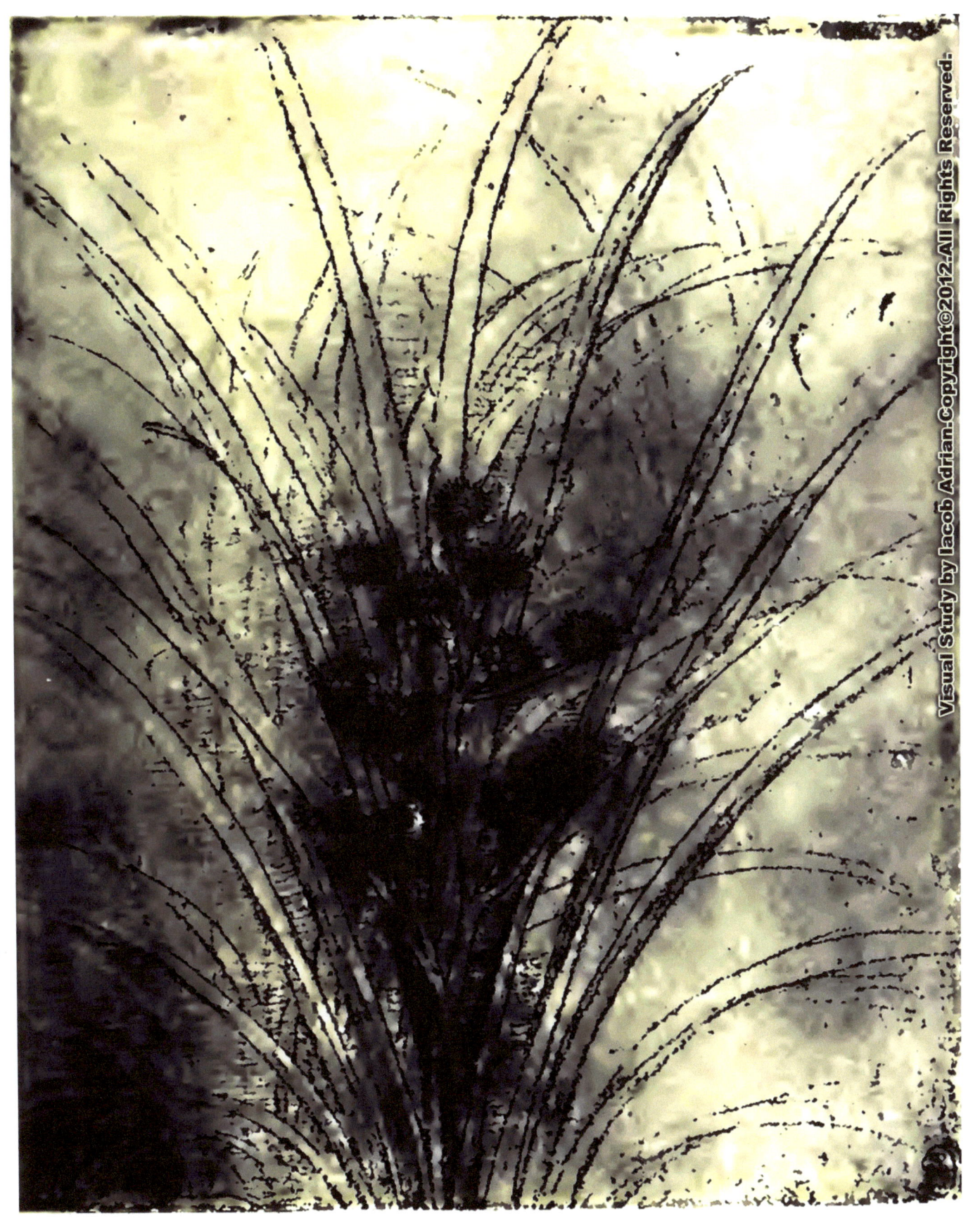

SPARGANIUM ERECTUM L.

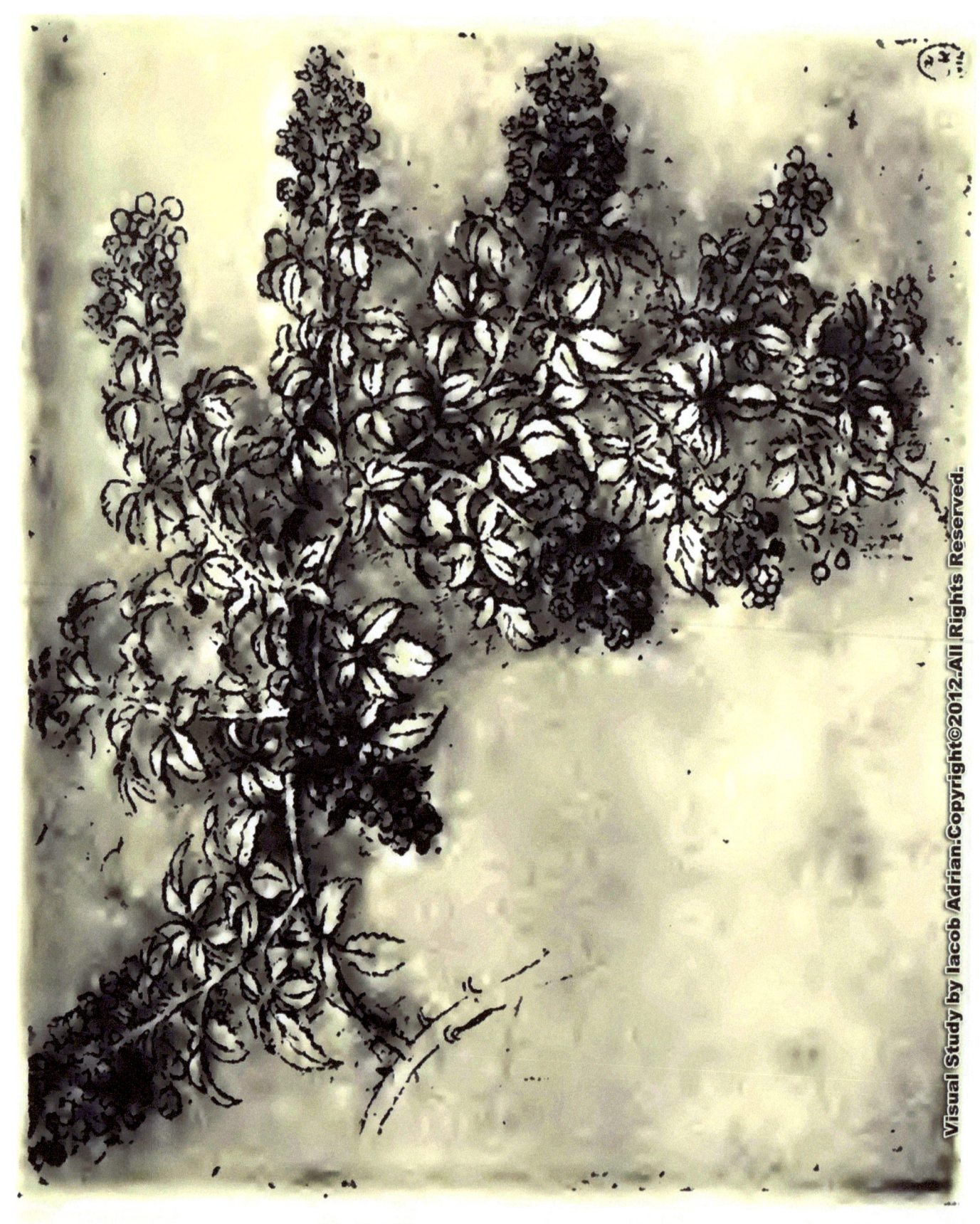

RUBUS IDAEUS L.

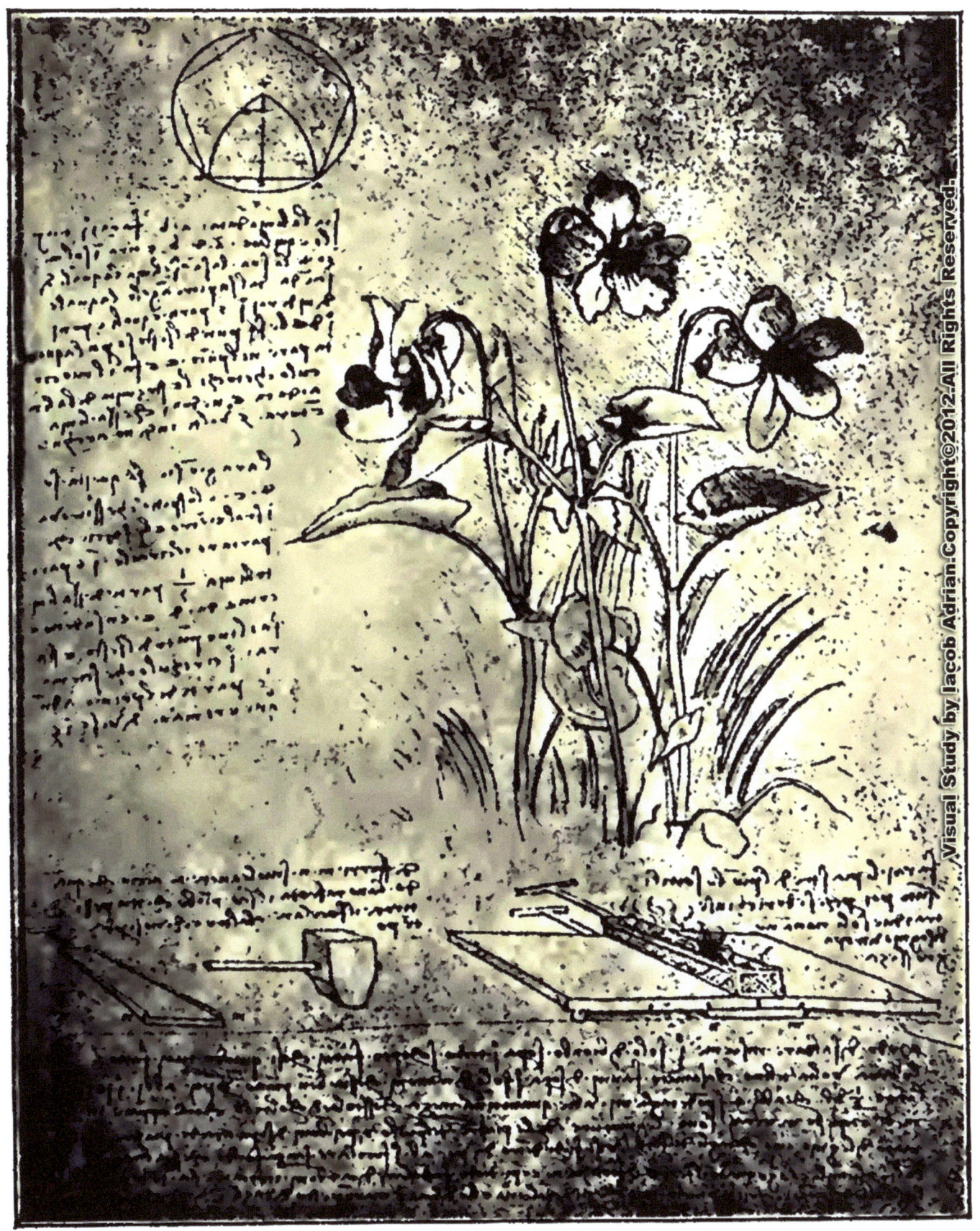

VIOLA (canina L.)

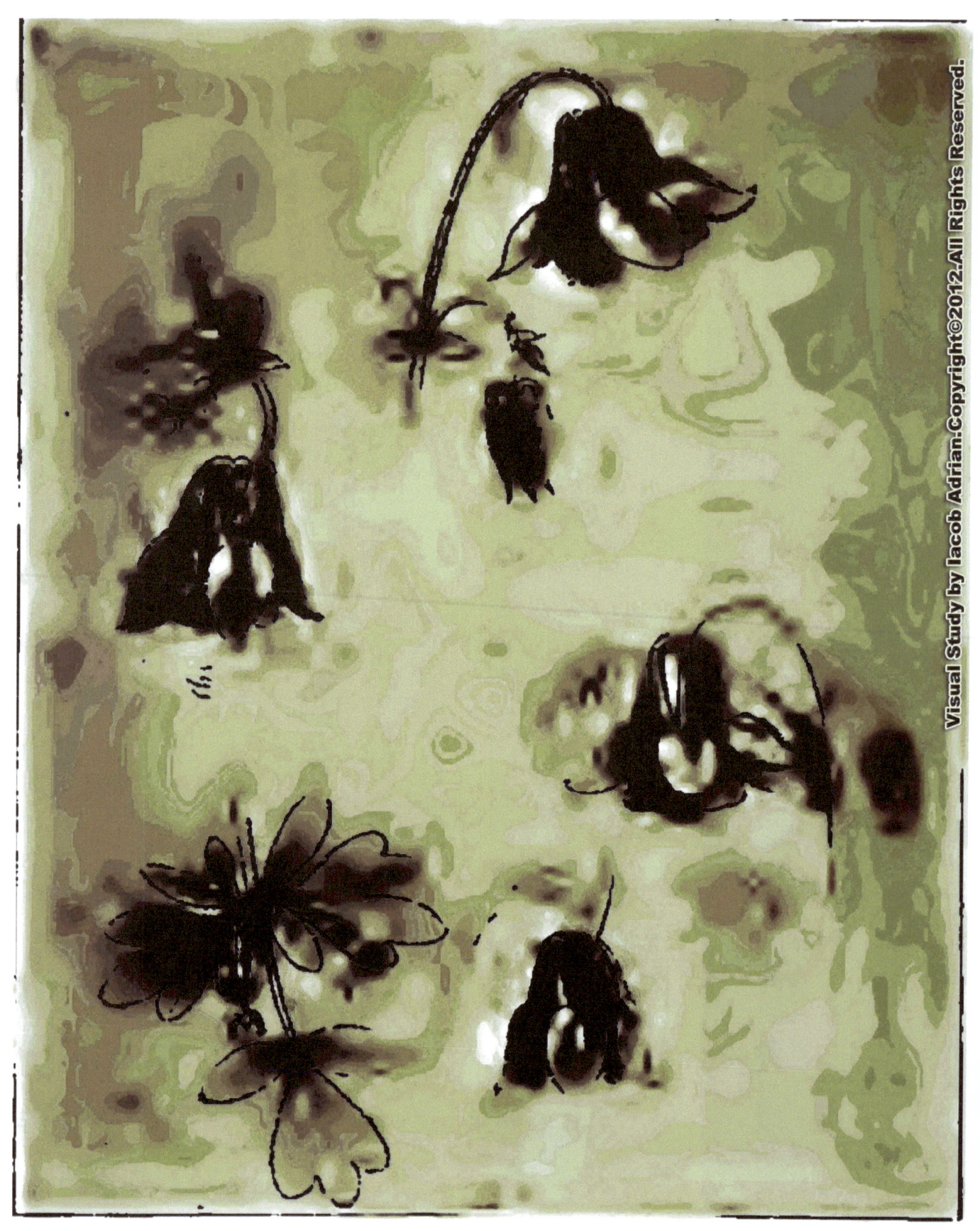

STUDIES OF FLOWERS AND LEAVES

Bibliographic sources :

Le piante e gli animali in Leonardo da Vinci (1922)
Author: Toni, Giovanni Battista de, 1864-1924
Publisher: Bologna : N. Zanichelli

Drawings of Leonardo da Vinci (1907)
Author: Leonardo, da Vinci, 1452-1519; Hind, C. Lewis (Charles Lewis), 1862-1927
Publisher: London G. Newnes

Leonardo da Vinci, artist, thinker and man of science (1898)
Author: Müntz, Eugène, 1845-1902
Publisher: London : W. Heinemann; New York, C. Scribner's sons

Leonardo da Vinci : (1920)
Author: Leonardo, da Vinci, 1452-1519; Zoege von Manteuffel, Kurt, 1881-1941
Publisher: München : H. Schmidt